with best wishes

the Sporting Cartoons of

ALASDAIR HILLEARY

With all my love
for Fiona, Flora, Rosannagh and Geordie.

First published in the UK in 1997 by Swan Hill Press,
an imprint of Airlife Publishing Ltd.

British Library Cataloguing-in-Publication Data
A catalogue record for this book
is available from the British Library

ISBN 1 85310 598 8

Typeset by Livesey Ltd, Shrewsbury, England.
Printed in Hong Kong.

Swan Hill Press
an imprint of Airlife Publishing Ltd.
101 Longden Road, Shrewsbury SY3 9EB, England

CONTENTS

FOREWORD

by Malcolm Innes

Some would argue that Loon and Loon's book do not need an introduction, that he is already a household name and quite capable of introducing himself. Perhaps he is too modest, not, as Churchill said of Attlee, with 'plenty to be modest about' as Loon's career is a genuine Highlands' success story.

He had thought in terms of asking a Royal to write this foreword, as he had drawn pictures of one or two in his time. Apparently one Royal had been to the same school (Gordonstoun) and also painted a bit, for things like postage stamps in the UK and ski-passes in Klosters. It never occurred to Loon for one moment that Royals' diaries are filled up months, sometimes years in advance and that they cannot just drop everything, even to help an old acquaintance. So he settled for his London 'agent', too solid to be a ghost-writer, but at least prepared to spend time proof-reading and correcting the author's phraseology and spelling.

*Loon's talent as an artist is only half inherited. Ruaraidh (*sic*), his Father, for his art exam at Eton during the latter stages of the last War took a blank canvas and painted it completely black. When asked what his efforts were meant to portray, he explained, I call it 'The Blackout'. The result? No marks on his scoresheet, six on his posterior. His Mother, on the other hand, is a descendant of James McNeil Whistler.*

Loon loves travelling and recording new places. He is a very international cartoonist. One of his first major commissions was to paint a picture for the St Moritz Tobogganing Club to mark the centenary of the Cresta Run in 1985. It combined individual portraits of sixty-four of the leading lights in the club at that time and was deemed a huge success. I was rash enough to lend my toboggan to him on the occasion of his first ride from the 'top' and saw a thoroughly hairy and painful horlicks being made of the upper banks. Last year, though, Loon won a 'guessing' race, estimating to within one second the time he would take from Junction to Finish. On the whole, he should have stuck to skiing. Scion of the Olympian Mackintosh tribe, he won the Army Downhill and Slalom competition and came second in the Army championships as a young Scots Guards officer in 1975. He is still, approaching middle age and maturity, no mean performer as a trick-cyclist on and off the piste.

Loon's private life leaves very little to be desired. Most of the time he lives on the Black Isle with his wife, Fiona, two daughters and a son, who calls me 'Minnis'. The Hillearys' honeymoon lasted a bit longer than most. They spent two-and-a-half years travelling and exhibiting their way around the world. They also have a house round the corner from ours in Clapham. Shortly after moving in, they were faced with dry rot in the roof and the water supply being turned off. Unknown to me (and, presumably, Fiona), Loon made an arrangement with my wife whereby he could use our 'facilities' during breaks from the studio. The first evening I got home my son Robert, then between 3 and 4, greeted me at the door with the news, 'Daddy, Mummy's got a boyfriend'. We never heard where Fiona went for her visit to the loo, but women are more discreet about such matters.

This book contains some of the best of Loon's work over the last twenty years. His success as a cartoonist, very much in the mould of Bateman, Thelwell and Giles, obviously owes much to his skills as a draughtsman and he nurtures the ambition to improve all the time and evolve an individualistic and classic style. Looking back over the years one can see how this ambition is being fulfilled. He is blessed with a varied, if sometimes outrageous, imagination and humour, his pictures are all about things he enjoys, as it is only by depicting such subjects that humour comes to the fore. We readily identify with his work which evokes spontaneous laughter. Not like another Scottish comedian whose performance was greeted by a pretty stony silence and the following conservation:

'Dae ye think he's funny?'
'Aye, I think he's funny.'
'Then how dae ye nae laugh?'
'Because I don't like him. I laugh when I get hame.'

We have had the misfortune of having the next-door stand to Loon's at the Moy Game Fair in Inverness-shire on more than one occasion. Point-scoring was inevitable. Twice I returned, after short breaks from minding the shop, once to find our sign-board upside-down, another time turned back to front with the words 'Gone Fishing' written in the joker's inimitable handwriting. We replied by adding the words 'Never knowingly oversold' under his board. It took him three hours to discover why everyone was pointing and laughing, less to detect the perpetrator.

In spite of everything, Loon is a good friend to many. He and his pictures, timeless and non-political, are universally popular. Loon is loyal to the extent of laughing at bad jokes. He has raised a substantial amount of money for Scottish Charities through his efforts on the 'Highland Cross', involving 20 miles of running and 30 miles bicycling over some of Scotland's least flat terrain, and through the sale of Loch Ness Monster droppings @ £6.50 a stool + £1.00 p and p. I am sure we all wish him and his publishers luck with his first venture as a combined cartoonist and author. Many will be pleasantly surprised by this proof that he can in fact write as well as paint.

Malcolm Innes

FISHING

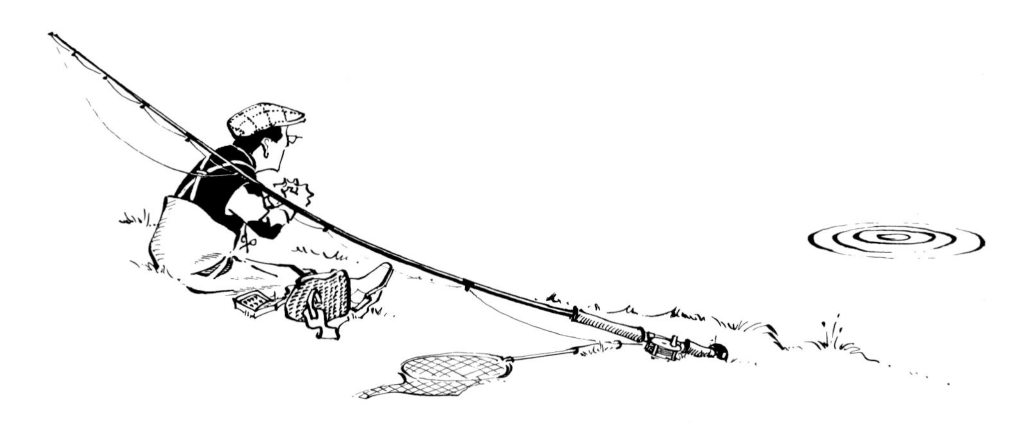

Smoked Salmon (Opposite page)

Without doubt the salmon is the King of fish. In this picture I have extended my respect to these magnificent creatures by including them in that wonderful moment at the conclusion of a really good dinner when the 'boys' gather round the port and set fire to a huge cigar.

The model for my picture was a fresh cock salmon obtained from the Conon River. On my drawing table, using a system of pulleys, props and supports, I managed to get this slithery salmon to adopt the five poses required for my picture. I also used one of my Monte Cristo No.5s and plugged it in this poor fellow's mouth. (I later ate the salmon and smoked the cigar!) The caption was obvious.

For many years my parents took us skiing. In order to fund some of these expensive trips, our suitcases were often lined with smoked salmon which my enterprising father would then flog to the hotels. In those days smoked salmon sold for a very high price. We always hoped that one or two sides remained unsold as it is such a treat to eat smoked salmon. On one occasion he was caught when the Customs impounded a suitcase packed with fresh grouse. By the time he had recovered them ten warm days had passed. The smell was indescribable! He also managed to smuggle a rucksack full of smoked salmon across the pass between Zermatt and Cervinia in order to extend his marketing range.

SMOKED SALMON

Watcha Cock!

True sportsmen are these two. They eat, sleep and drink their sport.

'Hey, Look, it's Hairy Mary!'

I wonder what the man who named the fly 'Hairy Mary' was thinking of. It is probably better not to draw attention to Mary's bottom.

A Wee Word of Thanks (Opposite page)

This man has just enjoyed a huge amount of sport. To have ten fresh fish on the river bank before the end of a day is a dream come true. He must have done something right as even The Almighty has allowed himself a peek at the scene. There are a million things in life which can uplift the heart but here on the riverbank shafts of sunlight pierce the billowing clouds, spring has arrived and with it a fresh run of fish. This scene was painted on the Beauly River and if it had happened to me I would probably still be on my knees.

A WEE WORD OF THANKS

Pickled Herring! (Opposite page)

A quick visit to the pub before Sunday lunch does wonders for oiling up the system. After a couple of pints of the landlord's best, ones legs take on a kind of floppy feel as if you were being supported by a fishes tail! The old lobster's bar-takings have been brisk but he's keeping a beady eye on general proceedings; after all nobody's going to mess with those big claws.

A herring fried in butter and oatmeal takes a lot of beating, but one thing that does is a pickled herring! Choose only the best from Scandinavian smörgåsbord with a shot of ice cold vodka and a slab of black bread!

These 'gourmet' paintings sometimes do not work out quite as planned, as the plate of fresh 'silver darlings' who modelled for me, were left over the weekend in a warm studio! What a shame we never got to eat them.

The Bottom

We took our family to the Turks and Caicos Islands for one of those wonderful Caribbean holidays. I spent many hours under water either with scuba gear or snorkel and was mesmerised by the fabulous colours of the fish, corals and water, in particular the ways the shafts of sunlight cut through the water and shimmered on the white sandy bottom. Sometimes in the myriad of marine life a large barracuda fish would appear and send us all scampering for the shore. Their reputation for ferocity is probably unfair but we weren't going to risk it. There is, however, one portly gentleman who is blissfully unaware of the danger lurking on the bottom as he puffs on his pipe and sups his rum punch. He floats along in a rubber ring with his bottom dangling like a full udder. It presents a target, in an inviting manner, to the speculative predator below. I painted this picture partly on the beach and partly by diving down to check on the colours and the shafts of sunlight.

'PICKLED HERRING!'

Time Out

If you were sitting in that boat, what would you rather be doing?

Fly Tying (Opposite page)

It's not often that I allow myself the dubious pleasure of indulging, once again, in schoolboy humour but this one just had to be done. I got into terrible trouble for drawing a caricature of my Adjutant in the Scots Guards who had given me what I considered to be an unreasonable quantity of extra pickets. He was depicted stark naked with his willy tied in a knot and dragging two heavy balls behind him. The picture was passed around the mess and, having had the desired effect, then found its way back to my lodgings where it fell behind a chest of drawers. It was discovered a few years later by the parents of a lovely young girl who had come to share the house. It was a moment that I would rather forget!

These two salmon flies are painted from those well dressed and colourful nineteenth-century flies. One can sympathise with the unfortunate situation in which one of these chaps apparently finds himself as he is firmly gripped in the jaws of a vice. (This is maybe a tip for us all to avoid vices.) Carrie Peto has framed this picture with feathers and various fly-tying instruments fastened onto the mount and it looks spectacular.

FLY TYING KIT
Loon!

I Wonder What the Boys are Doing Now?

This was a commission for a leaving present to Lord Keith who was greatly looking forward to a little bit of fishing in his retirement, leaving his directors to carry on the job in hand.

Yah Boo! (Opposite page)

I have a pair of very baggy waders and there was an occasion on the Ness River when the fish were jumping all around me but nothing would take. One of these fish jumped right beside me and I thought for a moment that I might have caught him down my trousers! There is nothing more frustrating than to spend the whole day flogging up and down the river catching nothing yet having them jump all around you. This scene is painted on the Beauly River but the salmon was painted in my studio. The mocking expression on the salmon's face is in fact my own as I used a mirror. If someone had watched me painting this they would have left in little doubt as to why I'm called Loon!

Overkill

When you know they are there and there is nothing in your fly box which will entice them out then perhaps it is time for the extreme.

Mmm! . . . Pheromones! (Opposite page)

I broke my Achilles tendon recently and was unable to take to the hill for our week of stalking at Shiel deer forest in September, so I decided to concentrate my efforts on the river. On Sunday evening I tied an outrageously colourful fly which featured a carefully chosen tuft of my wife's pubic hair (theory being that pheromones might work as well on the old cock salmon as they do on me). Fiona dismissed the idea as absurd and a waste of time, BUT on Monday morning on my eleventh cast I hooked and landed a beautiful 4lb fresh fish! My euphoria knew no limits!

The problem was not so much that I was running out of raw materials (Common Market practice of 'set aside' was applied), but what to name this phenomenal new fly: so I wrote to the Field *to see if some of their readers could help (Fiona insisted on my letter being anonymous). The replies came flooding in, most of which were unprintable, and offered us many possible names such as Appetiser, Dog Nobbler, Missionary, Woolly Bugger, Hairy Mary (or more appropriately Fiona Mary), Mountain Damsel, Hot Cat, Fuzzy Wuzzy, Pussy Allure, Angler's Tail, or as one reader suggested a collection of hair from various donors could be called Pussy Galore, but my favourites were Lunar Rise and Magic Merkin (a merkin being a pubic wig). Other suggestions included Curly Whirly, Black Puss (or blond, red, brunette etc.), a Wifey's tail or an Old Wives Tail, the Pubic Tube, Ginger Quim, Quimsy Whimsy, Fanny Craddock, Shiel Snatcher, Loon Puller, Shielagh, L'Unique (but this reader wanted to know if it was a dry fly or a wet fly!), Fanny's Fancy, Supreme Temptation, Pub Grub, Garry Clitter, Nympha Pubis, Bald Fanny, or Patience, but it was originally entered into our fishing register as having been caught on a Clitter! I received one wonderful note addressed to ANON from a dear friend, the late Geordie L-M. as follows:*

If you are the bloke whose tendon was broke
and who wrote to the Field *t'other day,*
You probably think you stand on the brink
Of finding the lure of which fishermen pray.

Now it's all very well to think you can tell
Which pheromone fashions a fly masterpiece,
But if it's your wish to catch a HEN fish
Why not try a piece of your own matted fleece!

"MMM! ... PHEROMONES!"
Loon

La Poissonnerie

If you've just had a day's fishing you can't very well arrive home empty handed.

Tight Lines (Opposite page)

Touch wood, I have never yet cast a big, juicy salmon fly and caught it in my ear but I know someone who has! It is really quite an achievement for me to fish for a whole day and not to lose at least half-a-dozen flies somewhere in the surrounding vegetation. I remember fishing on the Carron with Jean Matterson and a fellow guest caught a cow on his back cast. The cow was somewhat startled and set off across the field with the fisherman in hot pursuit not quite knowing how to deal with the situation. He later retrieved his fly but the hook had straightened itself out. His entry in the fishing register later that evening was 'Had cow on the line but, lost it'. Meanwhile back on the riverbank our fisherman has hooked the tree tops just as he was aiming gently to land his fly on the nose of a nice fresh fish. To rub salt into the wound, the fish will probably rise again with a grin on its face.

Loon ©

Birds One, Humans Nil

It is a fantastic sight to watch an osprey catch a fish. But did he really have to choose the one that you were about to hook?

A Fine Catch (Opposite page)

Whilst fishing on the Conon River, Melfort Campbell persuaded me to sit in a large fisherman's rubber ring and floated me off with my fishing rod to fish the pool. This contraption had been made for fishing in areas which were impossible to reach from a boat. I soon realised that it was very difficult to steer and before I knew it I was bumping down the rapids. I reached the next pool below and decided to have a cast. At that moment I got the shock of my life when a monster of a fish jumped out of the water right beside me. This whole scene seemed to cause great amusement to the assembled company. When we stopped for lunch, Melfort told me that only the day before, from the very same spot, a lovely eight-pounder had jumped into his boat. Every now and then we need a bit of luck whilst fishing and this chap is getting more than his fair share as a nice fat fish flies over the waterfall straight into his net.

Loon

THE SUMMER SEASON

Expectations

I was once invited to play a round of golf on the Championship course at Royal Sandwich and was the first person to tee off after Sandy Lyle had won The British Open there. I had been asked to play by an upstanding member of the club who was under the impression that I was a competent player. I strode boldly forward, confident that my ball would fly as well as the very best. I teed up, took my stance, addressed the ball and, choosing a spot well into the distance, wound up my club and like a coiled spring and swung with every ounce of energy God gave me. Such was the force of my attack that my whole body was left in a very unnatural position as the realisation slowly dawned on me that the ball still sat happily on the tee. My feelings of confidence underwent a complete metamorphosis and if ever I had wished that the earth would open up and swallow me that moment was it. I eventually connected and sent my ball tottering weakly down the fairway, to the acute embarrassment of my host. Several times during the round, as I hacked at the beautifully groomed turf, he whispered politely that perhaps it would be better if I picked up my ball and walked with it for a little way. For some reason he has never asked me back again. In this picture not only have I tried to suggest how confident the player is feeling but also what the playing partners expect to see. It's a very humbling game. One day you think you have mastered it then the next it's back to square one again.

THWAK!
1st HOLE
575 YARDS

The Ascot Rat

This was the picture that set me up as a cartoonist. I showed it to Oliver Swann and Charlie Fortescue, now Ebrington, who gave me my first exhibition on leaving The Scots Guards. The exhibition was called The Ascot Rat *and we sold everything in two days.*

She's as Lame as an Old Donkey (Opposite page)

Royal Ascot, apart from being one of the highlights of the English social calendar, has some of the best racing of the year and in this wonderfully colourful scene there is a moment of great anticipation as owners, jockeys and trainers foregather in the paddock prior to a big race. After months of careful preparation the trainer, with the humour of a wicked Irishman, breaks the shattering news of how this heavily fancied runner is as lame as an old donkey. His answer is 'bute' (phenylbutazone), which is a good equine pain-killer.

"SHE'S LAME AS AN OLD DONKEY... BUT WE'VE TOPPED HER UP WITH BUTE!"
Loon

The Fourth of June – or thereabouts

It is one of the great and classic scenes of an English summer to see the procession of boats at Eton College, especially when the cox and oars stand up and shake the flowers from the boaters into the water (sometimes they topple over and follow the flowers in). One of the more ridiculous sights is seeing the little darlings being got ready by their adoring mothers.

The Water Jump (Opposite page)

The biggest crowd puller at Badminton is the water jump and it never fails to provide plenty of entertainment. For some competitors there is an inevitability about this obstacle.

CLEAN TOWELS
WET CLOTHES
Loon.

Golf Balls

You hear it all at the nineteenth hole.

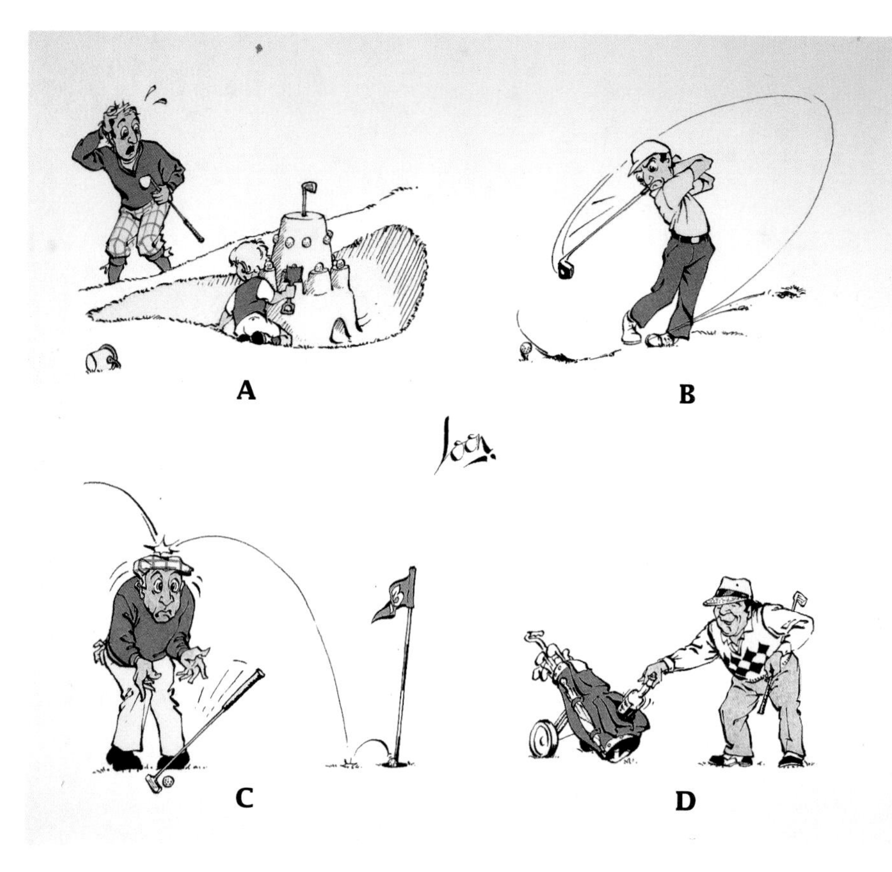

A ***Bunkered***
Daddy, daddy look what I've made!

B ***The Air Shot***
That's impossible.

C ***In Off the Red***
It's a hole in one.

D ***The Tipple***
This will improve my game.

Tennis Ball (Opposite page)

The real test for a vaguely risqué *piece of work is for me to show it to my mother. When I tried this one out on her I thought she was going to have a hernia as she laughed so much, which says something about her sense of humour as much as mine. I have to say that this is one of my favourite jokes, but there are one or two people in this world that I would not dare show this picture to, so if they happen to be reading this piece then look away. I must also point out that, contrary to popular belief, this is not a self-portrait.*

Loon ©
"HE SAID THAT THING IN HIS POCKET WAS A 'TENNIS BALL' ~
..MY DEAR THAT MUST BE PAINFUL, I'VE HEARD OF TENNIS ELBOW!"

Coming Out On Top

I believe the modern idiom is vertically challenged, but for this little Ascot rat nothing will hold him back as he watches his horse romp home to win.

Emergency Rations

I suspect this is not the first emergency he's had, but he's chosen his moment on an important putt to steal his wee tot.

The Lob (Opposite page)

I find one of the most fun shots to play on the tennis court, which drives my wife mad, is to smack the ball practically into the stratosphere. This may entail the sacrifice of a needed point in a set of tennis but, my goodness, it is satisfying. Just imagine doing this on the centre court at Wimbledon when the ball interferes with air traffic control and comes down somewhere near Hyde Park.

THWAK!
'THE LOB'
Loon.

The Outsider

It's a winning ticket. Whenever I go racing I always imagine that it is going to be me.

The Favourite

In a sea of happy faces, when everybody has chosen the winner, there is generally one unfortunate man who got it wrong.

Cricket Cap (Opposite page)

A village green in England on a hazy summer afternoon with the gentle thwack of leather on willow is one of the more pleasant scenes I have been lucky enough to experience. In a similarly relaxed vein our hero, by offering his cap, has not only saved six runs but also caught the batsman. (This is in fact illegal under the Rules of Cricket.)

Loon.

STALKING

There's A Man With 'Bloody High' Pressure

I used to stalk on Kingie beside Glen Quoich and learned much of the skills from a man named Alec Boyd. He had a son named Farquhar whose reputation went far and wide and spread fear and trepidation in all those folk who stalked for only a few days each year. For Farquhar Boyd, who now lives in Australia, was the fastest and fittest man that ever scaled the Scottish hillsides and many a person who, whilst following him, has wondered where on earth their next breath will come from. We used to try anything to slow him up with comments such as 'Excuse me Farquhar, (gasp) but I think I have (gasp) just seen some hinds' or 'Farquhar, who stalks the land to the west?' or even 'I think I'm seeing some hikers'. This at least gave one the chance to catch one's breath, but more dramatic comments such as 'God, I think I'm going to die' or 'Farquhar please stop' had absolutely no effect on him whatsoever.

Every year I promise myself to try to lose some weight before the stalking season begins as, in theory, the less weight I have to haul up the hill the more energy will remain before tackling the next but it never seems to work. Even the deer have noticed! My alternative caption is 'I do believe he has lost weight this year'.

In selecting the right stag to shoot, much thought and experience goes into assessing the weight and general condition of a beast and a good stalker will always be able to recognise the same stag one year to the next. Roles have been reversed here and the old puffing Billy is recognised by the stags as he returns for another year of gruelling exercise. My landscape is painted with the Five Sisters of Kintail in the background.

Safe Rutting

You can't be too careful these days. This is a new way of keeping the numbers down with a bit of free enterprise on the hill.

Stalking Times

Monarch of the bathtub (with apologies to Landseer). Stalking is the sport of kings. It's that lovely moment in life with a good hearty dram in a hot peaty bath.

Break In (Opposite page)

It is a sad reflection on the world today that many wild animals are being squeezed out of their natural habitat by the greed and needs of human beings. Even a plantation of conifers can occupy a favoured winter feeding ground for deer or it can block the access from one piece of land to another. But 'Oh, ho, ho, look what we have here?' This mischievous old beast has beaten the system; with a pair of wire cutters he and his kind will soon be tucking into a fine crop of young trees. It's the landowner's nightmare to think of the damage these animals can do to this valuable crop.

WIRE CUTTERS

Hind's Baked Beans

This is one way of repelling those amorous advances.

I Wouldn't Mind Culling That Lot (Opposite page)

I have a love–hate relationship with hikers. When high up in the hills I love them because of our mutual interest in the mountains. I hate them because they appear during the stalking season and ignore the signs that are put up asking them to contact the stalker. The deer cull is vital to the proper management of the estate and there are many jobs that depend on it. There is a very short season to achieve this and, as more and more people take to the hills, the cull is becoming more difficult. I painted this picture looking east towards Cluanie and had in mind the frightening figures of the world's population explosion and wouldn't it be ironic if the roles could be reversed and the deer could cull us. I am quite sure that they, like me, would begin with the orange cagoules, the mountain bikers and the ghetto blasters.

"I WOULDN'T MIND CULLING THAT LOT!"
Loon

Oh Deer!

One is not always successful out stalking and to be out-manoeuvred by a monster beast is enough to put the fear of God into you. It is rather like, as a child, running flat-out down the corridor convinced that you are being chased by a tiger.

Hide and Seek (Opposite page)

I was awoken at four in the morning from a deep sleep, having partyed into the wee small hours the night before, and after an obligatory cup of coffee we met our Austrian hunter and set off by car into the foothills of the Alps. In the blackness of the night we drove well into the forest, parked half-way up a hill and with still very few words spoken we quietly made our way with rifles, long poles and tracking dog by foot through trees and across hillsides until we eventually arrived at the hide. There was total silence, but as time ticked by the creatures of the forest slowly awoke. The light began to seep over the snow-capped mountains as we sat watching the world come to life. My eyes began to get heavy and thoughts of my bed lingered in my mind, the hunter puffed on his pipe and the dog lay sleeping as we watched the clearing in front of us where the deer might appear. All of a sudden the gentle silence of the morning was shattered by the most almighty roar that seemed to shake the very seat I was sitting on: it was like being plugged into the mains. The thrill shot up my spine, my eyeballs popped out and my ears opened right up as the echo bounced around the valley. I glanced at the hunter who remained totally unmoved by this experience and I later learned that the stag was still a good way off. This situation tickled my imagination and I straightaway recorded some ideas for cartoons in my little sketch book which always accompanies me. In this picture sleep has got the better of him. The massive forest stag is incensed by the insult and is at the point of omitting a roar from the very depth of his bowels.

Cliffhanger

Revenge is sweet. One only has to look at the prongs on his antlers to feel the impact.

The Final Approach (Opposite page)

As guests at West Glen Quoich, my brother-in-law, Evan Baillie, and I had a wonderful day's stalking together. By four o'clock I had a stag in the larder and was back in time to watch Evan stalking a large herd of stags that had recently crossed the march from Shiel to graze on the hillside above the larder. There were several shootable beasts amongst them and we could see the one that the stalker and Evan were going for. They were very close and had to stalk along a contour of an open convex slope. It was fairly shallow deer grass and in order to get close enough it required stealth and fieldcraft. All we could see from below was Evan's great backside slowly easing its way towards the deer. It was all the deer could see as well and enough to make them move to a position well above and out of shot of the stalking party who had not realised the situation. They provided endless amusement for us below and the whole scene demanded a cartoon.

We've Worked Hard For This One

This switchy beast is better off in the larder. Fergus Laing at the end of a great day's stalking.

He Missed (Opposite page)

There is nothing more demoralising than to miss. After hours of exhausting climbing, patient spying and careful stalking how could you make such a blunder? This has given the stags a great source of amusement and they are enjoying a really good laugh at your expense. Would it be too cruel to follow my father-in-law's advice and paint the pair to this picture calling it 'He Missed Again'?

"...HE MISSED!"
Loon

The Roar

One almost sure way of getting lost on the hill is to keep going when the mist comes down and it is sometimes better to sit down and wait for it to clear. The mist can also be useful in providing a cover for you to get in on some beasts, but the deer have an acute sense of hearing and the slightest strange sound, such as the tap of a stick on stone, will send them clattering off across the rocks. I have spent some very exciting days chasing beasts in the mist and it is even more exciting during October when the rut is in full swing for that is when the stags are roaring. Their roar is the most wonderful deep and reedy sound that comes from the bottom of their bellies. It is either a daring challenge to another stag or an exclamation of total male dominance. When you are not expecting to hear it, and a roar splits the air only feet away from you, it would put the fear of God into any human being. It is at this time of year that the behaviour of these magnificent animals in fighting to hold their own group of hinds strikes a chord in my heart, which sometimes gives Fiona cause for alarm!

Forty Winks (Opposite page)

The west coast of Scotland can provide some of the best stalking in the country and I have been fortunate enough to have enjoyed many wonderful days on my father-in-law's forest at Glen Shiel. The nature of the countryside does not allow for machinery and we still use ponies, in the traditional manner, to recover the deer. Our late stalker, Ian Campbell, bred the finest Highland stalking ponies in Scotland and I have learned a lot from him on how to handle them and break them in to carrying deer carcasses.

I have also learned what it takes to be a good pony boy; to know how far to bring the ponies so as not to disturb the stalkers and to know when and where they should be taken once a shot has been fired. This can sometimes take hours of waiting and if, on a dry, hot August day, you have enjoyed a can of beer with your piece, then it is only too tempting to let your eyelids close in the peace and tranquillity of a deserted glen. As the ponies peacefully graze and the burn babbles with the occasional bumble bee buzzing by, one is blissfully unaware of the impending wrath of a fuming stalker as he hauls down two stags on his back which were shot several hours previously high up on the tops. Perhaps to add to this impending explosion we see the blissful nonchalance of the Rifle as he strolls down the path, safe in the knowledge that he has done his bit.

The Walled Garden

With a hop, skip and a spring in the air, over we go for a feast of fresh veg.

The Stag Party (Opposite page)

When I was a young subaltern in The Scots Guards I attended several stag parties as various of my fellow officers fell by the wayside. They were all pretty wild evenings but none so much as the one for Julian Lancaster. Each stag around the table is based on a particular person. They know who they are but I will not name them. Things went from bad to worse when the lady of the night undressed revealing her shapely curves to the assembled company. Some passed out and others became legless as the port freely flowed.

BOLLY

Shooting

Bullshot (Opposite page)

Whoever invented bullshot should be awarded a medal as it is really one of the better moments of the day when this morale booster arrives. It is a glass of hot consommé and usually has a shot of vodka or sherry added to it. Apart from its sustaining effect it gives an opportunity for the Guns to get together and have a chinwag. A second helping will oil the conversation and time will slip by. It is quite possible that, whilst engrossed in this secret session, the beaters have started the drive and the pheasants have all slipped by in a victorious escape. This situation might test the patience of a head keeper who can see all his hard work legging it across the field.

AMH 90
Loon.

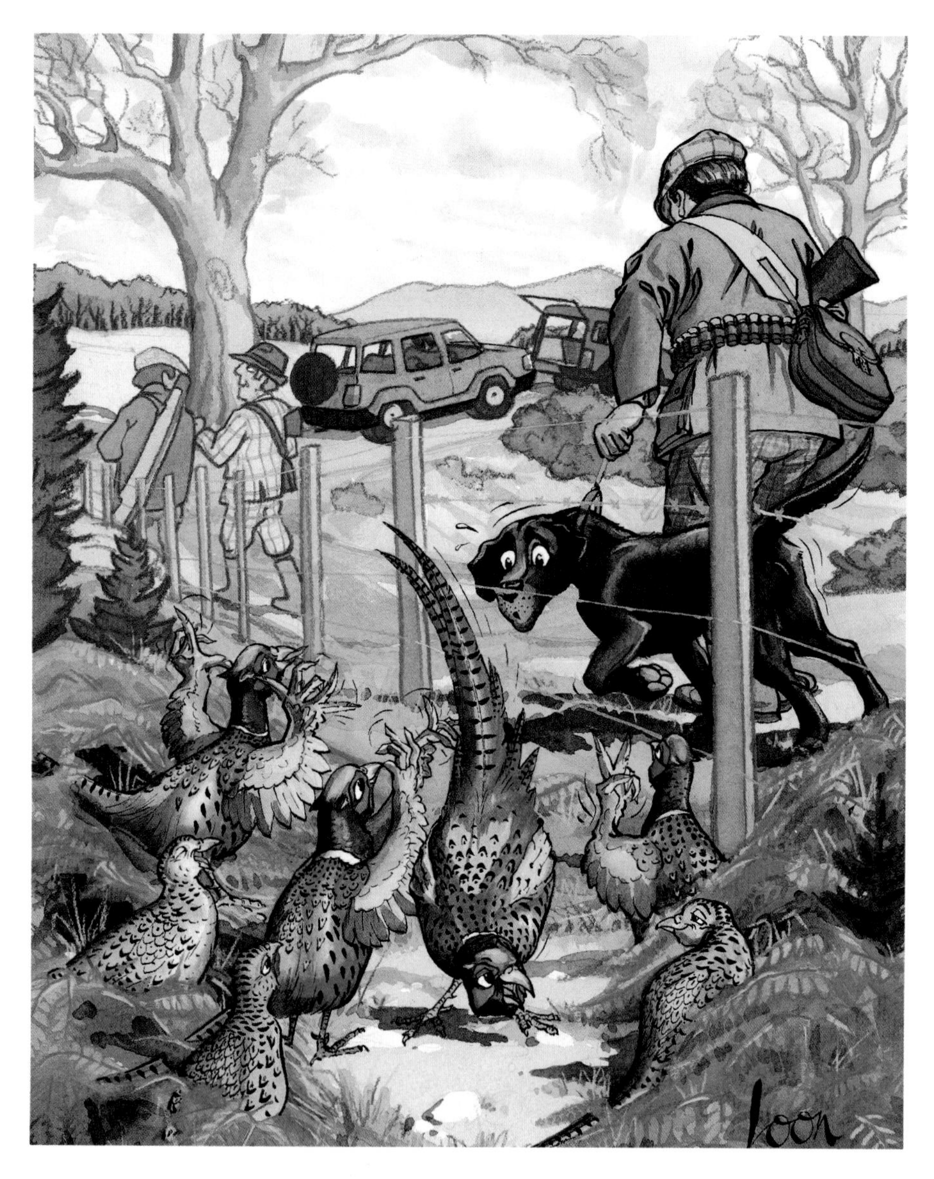

At the End of the Day

Even the best disciplined of dogs find it difficult to ignore some passing distraction, but here is a group of pheasants who have survived the drive and are thus able to 'cock a snook'.

Public Enemy Number One

These cheepers are learning a lesson of a lifetime but little do they realise that the shooting man is probably the greatest conservationist of them all.

Fly Past (Opposite page)

If it is a blue day and one has just enjoyed a good lunch then it is hardly surprising that one should want to give way to the soporific effects. For the poor old beater who has sweated his guts out only to be confronted by this sleeping sportsman is all too much as the grouse birds pour over his position.

4
Loon.

Champagne Shoot

The world record currently stands at 177 feet for firing a champagne cork out of a bottle but if you aim the cork carefully enough you could not only have pheasant for supper but also several glasses of bubbly.

Caught Short (Opposite page)

Before I was allowed to start shooting, many an August day was spent trudging the Morayshire moors as a grouse beater. We used to walk for miles through the long heather and peaty bogs in a supreme effort to get the coveys of grouse to fly over the line of butts. We paid great attention to who was shooting and many of them were the heroes of my youth and some of the finest shots in the land. Even such great figures have needs and may not choose their moments as carefully as they could. I don't know who is more relieved, the grouse or the grouse shooter. I have painted the landscape partly from memory, but I did also go up onto the hill in order to get the details and colours correct, which is something that I have always been keen to produce.

4

Selective Hearing

When there is game to be chased, even though it is in the middle of a drive, it's time for these disobedient dogs to protect their hearing.

Out of Season

There is a mistake in this picture. I wonder if you can spot it?

Charlie Fox's Feast (Opposite page)

We can hunt them, trap them, chase them or shoot them but really more than anything we admire them. One of Charles James Fox's famous repasts is freshly-shot pheasant, and here on this Boxing Day shoot a friend has been brought along to share and enjoy the quarry of our shooting friend. They cannot believe their luck as pheasant after pheasant drops like manna from heaven. We used this painting as a Christmas card for the Game Conservancy with the caption 'It Must Be Christmas Already!'

4

Oven-Ready

Some call it a hard mouth and others call it jolly good fun but this pheasant has more or less been plucked.

Quack, Quack, Grrrr

I can't go any quacker!

We're Not Flying in This (Opposite page)

Britain is not only famous for its superb pheasant shooting but it is also well known for its Union-based workforce, which has in the past been well practised in the art of going out on strike. In this cartoon the comrades sheltering from the snow are making it quite clear to the beater that today is not the day for flying. If the shop steward of this group of pheasants had been born with fingers, two of them would have been rudely presented to our startled friend.

WE'RE NOT
FLYING
IN THIS!
Loon.

Unseated

Somewhere lying in a ploughed field is the erstwhile resident of this shooting stick as the hare gallops off into the distance.

Scramble

'Time to get airborne, chaps, the enemy is on my tail.'

Over, Over, Over (Opposite page)

This is a drive on the back road to Dochfour on my father-in-law's land near Loch Ness. He can produce some of the most spectacular high and fast pheasants in the country and each drive is an experience to be savoured. If you are lucky enough to draw peg No.3 you will be in the hot seat but, on this occasion, every single pheasant in the covert flies in a steady stream over your peg alone and your infuriated neighbour can only shout 'Over, over, over' as you frantically fumble to load the cartridges which are quickly running out anyway. For a fleeting moment you wish you weren't there.

3

They're Surrendering

Those brutes, they have ruined our sport.

It's Rude to Point (Opposite page)

Consider first that man and dog have hunted together for many thousands of years and this symbiotic relationship has produced one extraordinary breed: the Pointer. The bizarre actions of a dog on point as it freezes rigid once it catches the scent of a quarry, are fascinating and very exciting to watch. Consider too the thrill of the sport as you close in with the Pointer, gun at the ready, to flush the game; the scene is as old as the hills! Can you imagine this scene being lost forever if hunting with dogs were to be banned. The last thing you expect in this ancient hunting partnership, is to share some of nanny's advice with an old cock grouse (maybe this is the origin of the word 'grousing')!

Not all of my paintings are done from life, but I did spend a very pleasant afternoon, with a hip flask up on the Lovat moor, to do this one. The theory being that after a midday nap in the fresh air, one's ability to carry out the job-in-hand is greatly enhanced; captains of industry take note!

"IT'S RUDE TO POINT!"

Sunday Visitors

Now this is a moment that our feathered friends will savour as they strut past kennels safe in the knowledge that the keeper is at church.

Last One Over the Line's a Chicken!

O.K., everybody, let's take number six. He hasn't hit anything all day.

Whose Dog? (Opposite page)

One has to feel very sorry for a host to see an out-of-control dog running in at the 'moment critique' and all the pheasants disappearing in the wrong direction, but it does make me laugh. His absolute exasperation at seeing his well-laid plans go totally awry is fully justified. Just occasionally the natural instincts of a shooting dog can get the better of him, as he totally ignores not only the cries and yells of his owner but also the months of hugely expensive training that have gone into trying to produce the perfect gundog.

HUNTING

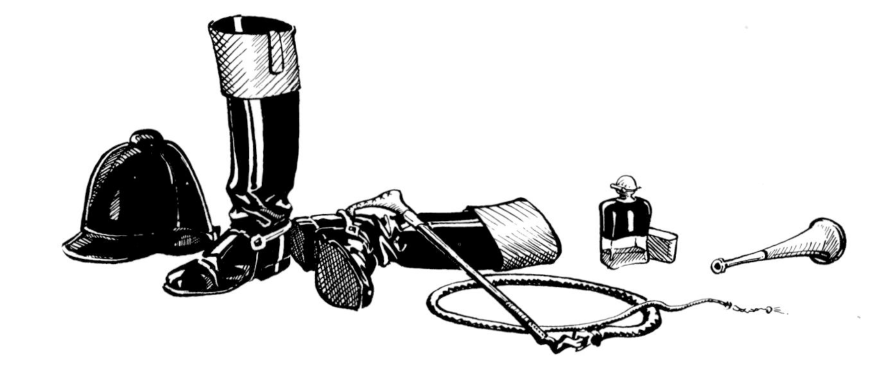

Charlie Fox's Stirrup Cup (Opposite page)

I came upon this idea whilst nursing a bit of a hangover; it was one of those mornings when I swore never to touch another drop! Had I really consumed all that booze or had I been led astray by some cunning and sly old waiter dressed in red? I sketched the idea into my little book where it matured for a number of months before being painted. My labrador made a rather reluctant model for me as she was manoeuvred around some slightly unnatural positions.

CHARLIE FOX'S STIRRUP CUP

Fresh Scent

I've always greatly admired any lady who hunts side-saddle; how immaculate they look. This foxy lady knows how to enjoy herself as, fresh from the hunt, she cracks a bottle of Château Sly. That's one habit she won't kick.

The Hunt Kennels

'Don't Overdo it, Charlie, they'll start begging next!'

Happy Days (Opposite page)

In reflecting on the essential activities of life, the six illustrated here would, to my mind, be hard to beat. I used to go shooting woodcock with my father and grandfather on Skye, where we would cover huge distances in all sorts of winter weather, but the real moment to savour was after returning home and having a bath to be seated in front of a peat fire, in dry clothes, with a large glass of whisky in hand.

3
Loon ©

Captain Ian Farquhar, M.F.H.

This man has that rare ability to hunt hounds and cross any countryside far quicker than anyone else. He took me round his kennels and then out hunting which was an experience in itself. My painting was a gift on his departure from the Bicester and Warden Hill Hunt.

In Harmony

I think that foxes enjoy hunting as well! Perhaps this is 'the unspeakable in pursuit of the uneatable'.

A Good Seat (Opposite page)

I have always admired riders who have a good seat. One way to do this is to follow on the heels of a young, well-proportioned filly at full gallop. It is wonderful to watch a good horseman stick like glue to his or her saddle over all kinds of terrain. I have often found this a little too difficult and come a cropper. Why, therefore, cannot some enterprising fellow invent a nice comfortable armchair which could accommodate an ample backside like mine, better shaped for the kilt than jodhpurs. After all, horses are dangerous at both ends and damned uncomfortable in the middle.

A GOOD SEAT

Weighing In

If he passes this one he's clinched it!

The Keith's Colours

He's eyeing up the horse and working out his tactics . . .

The Ultimate Insult (Opposite page)

I don't know whether old Charles James Fox conducted this business on a weekday or the Sabbath, but it is rather a lovely idea anyway. I had a fascinating conducted tour by Ian Farquhar round the Bicester Hunt kennels when I got an insight into the characteristics of bloodlines that had been bred into the pack. This helped them to become the ideal hound suited for that kind of countryside. To see them all 'on point' after a fox is one of the most exhilarating feelings that a sportsman can have. So what better way for our cunning old friend to give two fingers to the pack.

A Head For Heights

This monster is just number one. It's enough to blow the air vent out of your skull cap.

SKIING

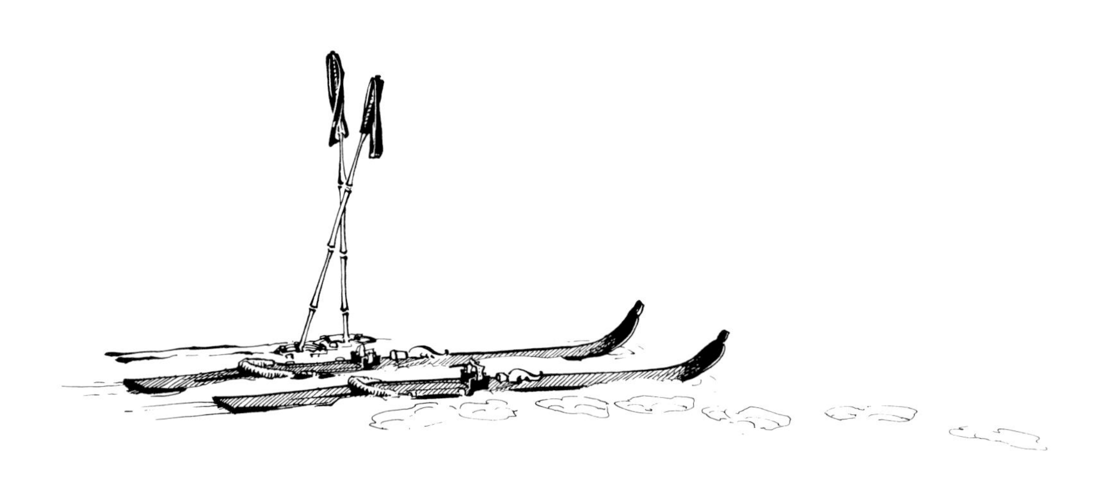

Sleighride (Opposite page)

Over 100 years ago two Englishmen were persuaded for health reasons to spend the winter at the beautiful spa town of St Moritz in the Engadine Valley. They returned with reports of weeks of unbroken sunshine, a magnificent Alpine landscape and exciting new pursuits: winter sports had begun. Today millions of people enjoy the thrills and spills of winter sports (some of whom have inspired my cartoons). The beautiful scenery, the mountains and frozen lakes however remain unchanged. In front of the town of St Moritz lies an enormous lake which freezes over and allows all kinds of activities during the winter months. There is polo, cricket, horseracing, langlaufing, walking and, of course, sleighrides. I painted this picture because I was so in awe at the enormous mountainous landscape of snow-covered trees in contrast to the tiny sleigh that jingled so peacefully along the frozen lake. There is a restaurant on the other side of the lake where they do excellent fondues. It is one of the most romantic things to return by horse-drawn sleigh all wrapped up warm against the freezing night air, with the town all lit up and set against the majestic mountains.

Stripping The Fir Cones
(To be read in a squeaky voice!)
Whilst racing with the army ski team I once miscalculated my cornering and did this with a slalom pole.

Heeeelp!

I think the anatomy is correct in this painting, the trouble was I couldn't persuade my wife to 'sit' for me! In fact she was the inspiration behind this catastrophe when she was caught short in the gum trees when we were skiing at Mount Buller in Australia; she finished up with a very cold backside!

The Engadine Marathon (Opposite page)

One of the most extraordinary and un-British sights in Switzerland is that of twelve thousand people cross-country skiing along a 42-kilometre course right down the Engadine Valley. The snaking line of steaming athletes crosses the frozen lakes like a column of ants. They glide effortlessly, but because they are so precariously balanced on their thin skis they occasionally get themselves into some wonderful tangles, often toppling over like little dominoes.

In painting this picture, the fantastic light and shadows of the mountains in the Engadine have been a great inspiration to me. I have brought in these absurd cartoon characters to bring some humour into the landscape and into an otherwise intensely serious and very Swiss occasion!

The Feel-Good Factory

Good times are just around the corner.

Crevasse'd (Opposite page)

I used to go summer skiing on the Kitsteinhorn Glacier in Austria and there was one T-bar that is now closed because a crevasse opened up underneath its path. The ski lift company built a bridge and if there was any occasion to give you the severe 'willys' it was to look over the edge of the bridge into the icy abyss. I remember the wonderful colours of the ice walls that became a darker and deeper blue as they descended into a freezing nothingness below.

The Black Run

Based on the Grand Couloir in Courchevel, the scene of some spectacular pile-ups!

Backscratcher

Up a bit . . . left a bitty . . . right a bit . . .
AAH! yes there!

Mountain Refuge (Opposite page)

As I woke up in the top bunk of a six-man 'couchette' I peered through the curtains of the train window to be struck by that blue sky and the magnificence of the snow-covered Alps; I was a young boy and I can still feel my veins racing with anticipation.

I had a similar feeling as I painted this picture. It was very exciting when confronted by a huge sheet of pure white watercolour paper; as you will see I have not covered much of the canvas with paint! A few trees, rocks and a patch of blue sky were carefully painted with strong colours of light and shade to contrast the awesome and magnificent whiteness of the fresh sparkling snow. All the time the fantasy grew of escaping into that wilderness, and as I painted that sweet little hut it felt like I really was there (and I wasn't 'tout seul' either)! I remember, also, when summer skiing in Norway, climbing along a ridge to discover a vast glacier of pure untouched snow and a perfect slope for almost half-a-mile; it made by heart leap for joy to ski it!

Signal

My old friend Timothy Laing had an outfit that I was rather envious of, but he did look a little like he had been squeezed out of a toothpaste tube!

The White Lady

There is a large mountain opposite the town of St Moritz, known as the 'Berg' and in certain light, at certain angles and with several glasses of 'Poivres Willheim' under your belt you too might see the fantasy spirits and naked figures that lie behind the vista! Look again.

Polo Dreams

It is amazing where you can go when sitting at a desk.

Dangerous Drop (Opposite page)

My mother once described skiing as the closest we can get to flying like a bird. To descend a slope with grace and speed is very exhilarating and one can become so absorbed that warning signs of an approaching precipice might pass unobserved. This fellow looks down the Engadine Valley as he clings onto the lone tree.

Beaver Creek

So that's what they get up to in the long winter months.

The Scissors

You could do yourself an injury doing this (snip, snip and Bob's your auntie!).

Let the Wind Blow Free (Opposite page)

'I don't think this is funny and I don't suppose you will either . . . but I can't help it!' This picture probably needs no explanation, as it is everybody's nightmare to be trapped with a farter in a cable car. Perhaps, because of the way it is painted, the observer might relate more closely to the perpetrator in the picture. I should maybe point out how much our brave offender is enjoying his crime; note the curled upper lip, flared nostril and also how the little finger of his right hand suggests the silent but deadly effects. This antisocial act on his fellow travellers has been utterly devastating. I have always loved this kind of humour ever since I was at prep school and I am sure that some people think that I have not progressed very far from those days.

Old Timer

He still has leather lace-up boots, hickory skis with cable bindings, bamboo poles and a favourite old hat and he's damned if he is going to change now.

Now That's What We Call Style (Opposite page)

These wild mountain goats have to be seen to be believed! The incredible ability of Steinbock to cling on to precipitous rock faces amazes us mere humans. They know of many terrifying gullies and coloirs where people fear to ski: so maybe we should allow the 'goat within' to come out and provide the required courage, confidence and style to tackle these extreme slopes.

So I wondered to myself what might impress these mountain goats as much as they impress me. Not only has our friend dressed himself in suitable attire but he is taking the steep powdery slope with the confidence and aplomb of the finest human skier and thus he has impressed even his own kind.

Chamois Country (Opposite page)

It is a great thrill to be able to spot a Chamois from a ski lift as they are very difficult to see. I sometimes wonder what makes these beautiful creatures climb to such heights and how they actually get there.

Springtime

Oompah, oompah, bang, bang, bang!
Let your udders swing and your bells go clang
Yodel up the valley, give your horn a blast,
And squeeze on the box, it's springtime at last!

The Thinker (Opposite page)

Did he or didn't he?
That is the question. Whether 'tis nobler to sit there and get a cold bum trying to work it out or to go off chasing a couple of saucy hinds is fairly obvious to me!

Snapped Shut (Opposite page)

The victim in this picture has actually queue-barged in order to get on to the chair-lift alone with this lovely blonde girl. In his rush to secure a place and with eagerness to impress and engage her in conversation, he has failed to position himself correctly on the chair-lift. She, meanwhile, has little patience for such advances and as she snaps shut the safety bar the stopper finds its mark and bang goes his manhood.

THE CRESTA RUN

Top's Open (Opposite page)

The beginner starts riding the Cresta from Junction, which is the easier part of the course and once one has achieved regular fast times you are allowed to go from Top (this is where the butterflies really take over!). Imagine that your name has just been called on the tannoy (butterflies begin to race around your tummy): you put up a hand in confirmation that you are ready to go (yet more butterflies). As you exhale one final steamy breath in the ice-cold air (and with it some of those butterflies hopefully) you crunch forward in the spiked shoes and crouch down to grab the toboggan. The barrier goes up . . . everything is ready as you very precisely lower your goggles (butterflies now gone ballistic) and take one final look from the top of the most famous iced run in the world! This is it . . . Top's open and you're off! Below you lies three-quarters of a mile of winding ice-track and banks (including the famous Shuttlecock corner) with a total drop of 514 feet, which you will cover at speeds of up to 80 mph.

The Cresta is the best known cure for a hangover, a physical state of affairs only too common in a place like St Moritz. I remember Rolf Sachs climbing up to Top Hut with me and issuing an almost incessant stream of complaints about how awful he felt and how this was not his day. I rode down the Cresta one ahead of him and, when he joined me at the finish, his face was exploding with excitement and he leapt up from his toboggan with a shout of: 'I feel great!'

Cresta Nightrider

She sometimes accuses me of snoring, or stealing the bedclothes, but surely riding the lower banks in my sleep is alright!

Since starting the Cresta in 1981 I have won two races, the 'Johannes Badrutt Memorial' in '95 (when I was given a superb handicap), the other was Dracula's Ghost Ride organised by Rolf Sachs. The latter race is run at night with flares marking the track and the winner is the one whose time is the nearest to a pre-chosen time; it is more of an excuse to drink vodka after lights-out!

People generally regard Cresta-riders as being a bit crazy; my suspicions were confirmed when Fiona and I were invited to join Rolf's party, going down the bobsleigh track on tea-trays at night. We formed a tandem with Fiona behind; all went well, but as we picked up speed, her grip began to tighten around my neck and the chin-guard of my helmet came up over my eyes, all I could see was the stars whizzing past as we tipped this way and that at high speed!

Shuttlecock

The one corner all riders fear is the safety valve of the Run and Shuttlecock Corner. For some people it is a dead cert, an inevitability, as they prepare to hurtle down the ice track. Riding my 'London agent', Malcolm Innes's go-fast weighted toboggan, I more than once exited the run in the famous Shuttlecock.

Early Morning Line Up

This is the sight that greets the early risers as the butterflies circulate in your stomach. The cold dry air and crisp squeaky snow promises another great day for riding! People sometimes ask me what the joke is in this picture as they begin to worry about their sense of humour; in fact there is no joke, so it is I who should be worrying about my sense of humour!

'To The Box, Dear Boy' (Opposite page)

'Debutantes' on the Cresta Run have to be dressed and ready to ride from Junction by 7.15 a.m. with leather knee and elbow pads, metal hand guards, crash helmets and special rakes on the boots. The Secretary, the flamboyant Lieutenant-Colonel Digby Willoughby MC, will call you to the box ready for your ride down. It feels as if one is committing oneself to something rather terminal as even Count Dracula, assisting as the Arbeiter, has come out to gloat at this ceremony.

CRESTA RUN
"...TO THE BOX DEAR BOY!"

The Running Start

What an embarrassing mistake or did he do this on purpose. 'Achtung, Schlitten!'

'Just What Did You Say, Young Man!'

(Opposite page)

Many people regard Cresta riders as complete nut cases and I cannot deny that there is a grain of truth in this. Our aim is to make ourselves go as fast as possible, up to 90 mph head-first down this icy course. However, there is a safety valve which is built in the form of Shuttlecock Corner with its shaved bank. If you do not know how to ride the Cresta properly or have taken a bad line then out you go. Although there is a nice soft landing in the straw this is where most of the accidents occur and consequently it is the best place to spectate and is known fondly as the vulture pit. It is also very near to one of the many paths on which, amongst others, prim old ladies and fur-coated princesses perambulate. So one can just imagine the horror as this Cresta rider's expletives split the air a little too close to one of our 'Grandes Dames'.

'Okay, Digby, Pull'

So here we are at the famous Shuttlecock Corner and the St Moritz clay pigeon club have found some new sport. Does Digby really know what's going on?

Rise

Rise is the name of one of the corners in the Cresta Run; however when riding the course, it helps to keep your mind on the job in hand. This picture is currently in the boot of someone's car as he hasn't yet dared to show it to his wife!

Battledore

If you are in the wrong place on this bank you're in trouble at the next because it's the famous Shuttlecock. This toboggan is currently travelling at about 75 mph.

'Go On, Fall, Fall, Fall'

Ghouls and blood-thirsty characters gather in the vulture pit for a ringside view of Shuttlecock Corner. People just love the blood and guts.

Ze Crazy Cresta

After riding, everyone foregathers in the Sunny Bar at the Kulm Hotel for prizegiving and a hearty, somewhat liquid lunch. One almost inexplicable ritual that Cresta riders perform, in six stages, is the action of a rocket. This is called a Firework. It begins with an almighty leap into the air followed by a cry of 'Boom' as you come crashing down. I often wonder whether the balcony is strong enough to take this combined assault from a Club with so many overweight members as ours.

A PUN IN THE OVEN

Hog'manay

Every porker in this picture was painted with someone in mind (some you may find more obvious than others) but I am not going to reveal the who's who.

The setting is no secret though. It is the Skye Gathering Hall in Portree. The Skye Balls are two consecutive nights of highland dancing and a wonderful gathering for a number of old Skye families. My family have been running them for almost 100 years now and I hope that one day I shall be allowed to take my turn (unless, of course, I have offended anyone!). Before the Gathering Hall was even built, the Brahan Seer (a man with second sight) predicted that a gathering hall would be built and that when its front doorstep was worn down to ground level the whole hall would tumble into the sea with everyone dancing in it. Only a lady wearing a red dress would be saved (see on the balcony). We had about 2½ inches to go and all looked well, then the Council resurfaced the area outside and brought the level up *so now there is about 1¼ inches to go. At least it makes us all dance as if each dance was our last!*

I took almost ten days to paint this picture and began by studying John MacKenzie of Gairloch's pigs at Conan Farm. I stood in the middle of the fold with these almost human porkers investigating everything from my feet up to as far as they could reach (my legs were held tight together!). Then back to my studio armed with my kilt, a mirror and plenty of ideas stored up, and I got down to work.

Hog'manay is a happy picture and I have tried to encapsulate the atmosphere and colour of this famous evening in the year. Perhaps it works so well because I not only know my subjects (the humans not the pigs) intimately but I also know the subject extremely well.

My pigs have also had another outing.

'HOG'MANAY !

The Name Dropper

If they have a title or pots of money he knows them.

Cashew Nuts

When we lived in Australia we had a pet cockatoo named Burton. He made the most dreadful noise, squawking around the house, and eventually Fiona said 'It's him or me'. He had an incredibly powerful beak which I am sure would have been capable of opening a tin of the most delicious cashew nuts.

Nanny's Day Off (Opposite page)

This brilliant idea for a cartoon was given to me by my old friend Tiffy Laing. He commissioned this for his wife, Charlotte, after a day of total exasperation with their four naughty children. Everything that could have gone wrong did go wrong and I've added in a few more things that were about to go wrong.

FART POWDER
JOBS TO BE DONE
CHARITABLE DONATIONS
MACANDREW + THICKY JENKINS.
GODFARVA
Loon.
IS A NEEdL NAddL GNOO.
DAY 1
NANNY'S DAY OFF!

The Morning After The Night Before

When the boys get together and make an evening of it there is always a price to pay. Breakfast for our Hereford bulls is not an occasion at the top end of the social calendar.

Spring in the Air

I would like to be able to say that this did really happen but the best I can manage is that it might well have done. I remember once strapping an alarm clock inside the captain of the guard's bearskin and set it to go off in the middle of the changing of the guard ceremony at Buckingham Palace with chaotic consequences.

The Board Meeting (Opposite page)

I have long had the idea of painting pigs in a boardroom and using the pun bore and boar. It was Andrew Caughey who commissioned me to reproduce the idea on paper and so followed a limited edition of prints. No self-respecting boardroom should be complete without this little piece of humour hanging on the wall.

So often the pressure on 'work' today seems to blot out the opportunity for humour and high spirits and this is where I find my role so important. Most of the figures in this painting are self-portraits as I reminisce about my days at Gordonstoun (generally spent in the back row of the classroom getting by with the minimum amount of work). Enough for now before I begin to 'bore' you myself.

LORD PIGLINGTON
OUR FOUNDER IS AN OLD BOAR
'HOGMANAY'
'PIGASUS'
MY SPEECH
THE 'BOARD' MEETING!

Are There Other Udders?

A nice, warm, full udder that swings from side to side would catch any passing bull's eye. For a more concentrated look at this phenomenon some enterprising old bovine has published the ultimate magazine – Udders *(this is also sold alongside Hugh Heffer's magazine called* Cowboy*). I am reminded of that old Yorkshire limerick:*

There was a mun from 'Uddersfield
Who 'ad a cow that wouldn't yield.
The reason why she wouldn't yield?
She didn't like her udders feeled.

Turkey And Plum Pudding (Opposite page)

In this picture Christmas turkeys are celebrating the fact that for once they get to eat the plum pudding and are not themselves brought out on a platter. Maybe one day this is what will happen if the animal lovers get their way. A neighbour of mine produced a splendid turkey for me to draw and I was impressed at how incredibly ugly these birds are. Their wattles grow when they get excited or angry and when you hear them gobbling away you understand how they have received the rather apt nickname of 'Bubbly Jocks'.

TURKEY AND PLUM PUDDING

Caviaaaaah!
Those little black pearls are pure unadulterated indulgence.

Sh Sh Sh Sch!
But champagne is an absolute necessity.

The Hen Party (Opposite page)

Having painted the very popular picture of 'The Stag Party', I thought that I should not be accused of being sexist and so came 'The Hen Party'. I have heard many stories, some more lurid than others, of the kind of things that women get up to on such an occasion and, knowing the extent that a man will go to in celebrating his last night as a bachelor, my mind boggles to think that the fairer sex might also go to similar lengths. The cockerel, seen here in such a tight pair of leggings that you could almost tell his religion, was based on one of my mother's pugnacious bantams.

The chickens, however, have a deeper connection. When Fiona and I lived in Spain, just after we were married, we rescued four hens from a battery unit and released them into our garden, which included herbaceous borders, an orange grove and a lovely swimming pool. The garden was tended by a wonderful Spaniard called Juan and we would all delight at the sight of these chickens as they enjoyed their new-found freedom. One particularly favoured pastime was when the hens would chase butterflies around the lawn. This involved running flat out zigzagging and snapping at the air behind the butterflies. I remember one afternoon hearing the most frightful commotion as one of the chickens had run full tilt into the swimming pool and Juan was urgently engaged in a rescue operation.

The Old Aunties

If you have ever heard the Australian kookaburra you will know why it is referred to as the laughing jackass. I think it sounds rather like two splendid old aunties sharing a filthy joke as they soak themselves in some lunchtime gin (I fear the left-hand auntie will rock right off the verandah with her next wicked one-liner).

Dinner is Served (Opposite page)

There are two aspects to this picture that I, and I expect many others, will be familiar. One is in appreciation for the amount of work that the lady of the house has put into producing a dinner party; please observe the anticipation that is welling up to bursting with her eager guests as they drool over the prospects that await them. The other aspect is the sheer delight of a young child as he discovers that when you pull one thing a lot of others seem to appear from nowhere and make a lovely tinkling and crashing noise. This is a game that even has splashes of colour to it as the creamy spinnach soup makes its mark on the pure white tablecloth. Here is a child who managed to escape from his cot to find out where all the action is, much to the amusement of the pictures on the wall. His high spirits would suggest that with good parental guidance he will grow up never to accept what is handed to him on a plate but to challenge it and find out what lies beneath.

This painting has been used on the front cover of the celebrity cook-book which raises money for The National Children's Hospital.

"...DINNER IS SERVED!"

TAIL PIECE

The Skye Man's Dream

It's a good life really.